That's HOT!

by Alison Auch

Content and Reading Adviser: Joan Stewart
Educational Consultant/Literacy Specialist
New York Public Schools

Spyglass BOOKS

COMPASS POINT BOOKS

Minneapolis, Minnesota

Compass Point Books
3722 West 50th Street, #115
Minneapolis, MN 55410

Visit Compass Point Books on the Internet at *www.compasspointbooks.com*
or e-mail your request to *custserv@compasspointbooks.com*

Photographs ©:
Two Coyote Studios/Mary Walker Foley, cover, 3; DigitalVision, 4; Two Coyote Studios/Mary Walker Foley,
5 (boy); Corbis, 5, (icicles); Two Coyote Studios/Mary Walker Foley, 6, 7, 8, 9, 11, 13, 14, 15, 16, 17, 19
(boy); DigitalVision, 19 (sand dunes); Corbis, 19 (snow scene); PhotoDisc, 20 (Earth); Corbis, 20 (icicles);
PhotoDisc, 21.

Project Manager: Rebecca Weber McEwen
Editor: Jennifer Waters
Photo Researcher: Jennifer Waters
Photo Selectors: Rebecca Weber McEwen and Jennifer Waters
Designer: Mary Walker Foley

Library of Congress Cataloging-in-Publication Data

Auch, Alison.
  That's hot! / by Alison Auch.
     p. cm. -- (Spyglass books)
Includes bibliographical references and index.
  ISBN 0-7565-0245-4 (hardcover)
  1. Temperature--Juvenile literature. 2. Temperature
measurements--Juvenile literature. [1. Temperature.] I. Title. II.
Series.
  QC271.4 .A83 2002
  536'.5--dc21
                          2001007341

Contents

What Is Temperature?

Have you ever been outside on a hot summer day? If so, you know about temperature.

Temperature is something you can feel. The temperature tells us how cool, cold, warm, or hot something is.

Hot

Cold

5

How Does a Thermometer Work?

We use a thermometer to **measure** temperature.

A thermometer has small lines and numbers on it. These stand for **degrees**. When the liquid in the tube gets hotter, it **expands**, and moves higher up the tube.

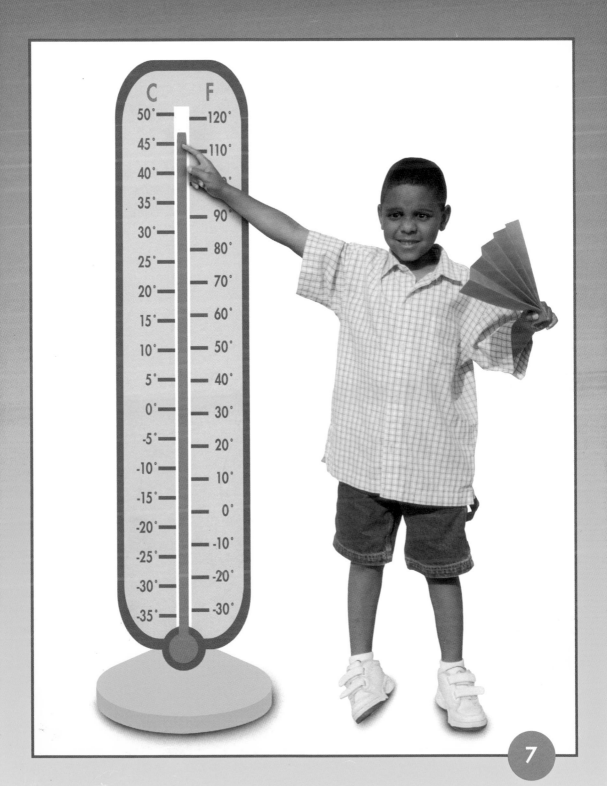

When the liquid in
the thermometer gets cooler,
it *shrinks*.

If the temperature is
falling, the liquid in
the thermometer drops
to a lower line.

Bath Thermometer

120
110
100   Hot
90   Warm
80   Tepid
70   Tempe
60   Cool
50
40   Cold
30   Bath
20   Freezing
10
0

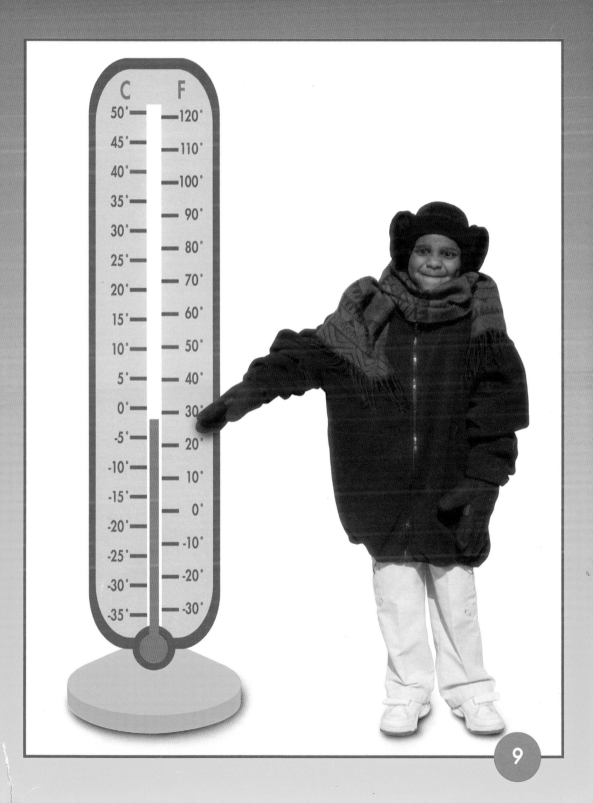

Celsius Versus Fahrenheit

There are two main ways to measure temperature: Celsius and Fahrenheit.

Celsius is used everywhere in the world except the United States. In Celsius, water freezes at 0 degrees. Water boils at 100 degrees.

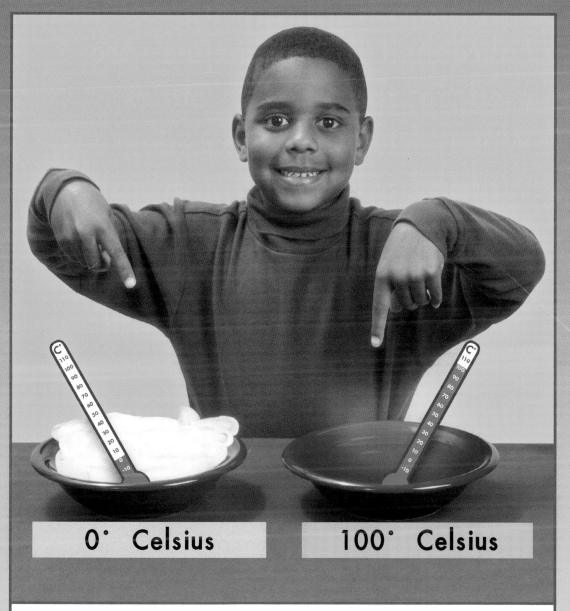

0° Celsius   100° Celsius

How Do You Say That?
Celsius: "sell-see-us"
Fahrenheit: "fair-en-hite"

Fahrenheit thermometers are used in the United States. Water freezes at 32 degrees. Water boils at 212 degrees.

Zero degrees Celsius and 32 degrees Fahrenheit feel exactly the same.
They are two different ways of saying the same thing!

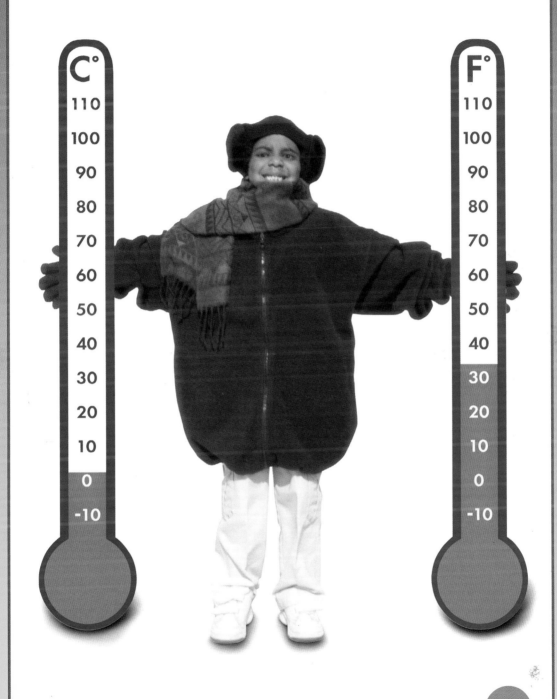

Temperatures
We Need to Know

Thermometers can measure the temperature of many things.

We use them to measure the temperature of water, food, and even our own bodies.

Body Temperature

The average temperature of the human body is 98.6 degrees Fahrenheit (37 degrees Celsius).

If a person's temperature rises, that person has a *fever*.

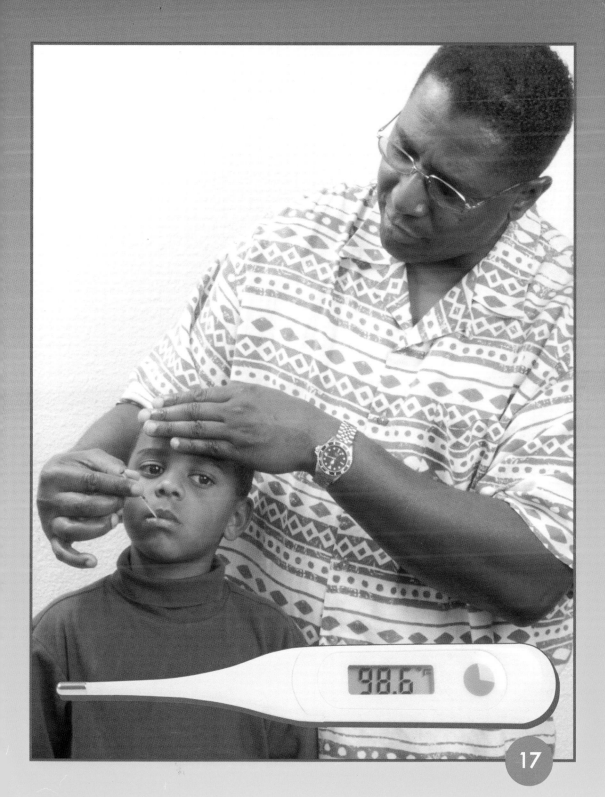

Temperature and the Weather

We also measure the temperature of the weather.

There are places where it is so hot it becomes dangerous. There are also places on Earth where it is dangerously cold.

Very cold or hot temperatures can hurt or even kill people.

Hot desert

Cold forest

19

Fun Facts

The average daytime temperature on Earth's moon is 212 degrees (100° C), but it gets colder than 200 degrees below zero (-129° C) at night!

In Antarctica, the temperature was once recorded at 128 degrees below zero (-90° C)! That is too cold for humans to *survive*.

The temperature of a lightning bolt is five times hotter than the surface of the sun!

Glossary

degree—one unit on a tool that measures something, such as inch marks on a ruler

expand—to get bigger

fever—a rise in body temperature above normal, often caused by an illness

measure—to find out the size or amount of something

shrink—to get smaller

survive—to stay safe and alive

Learn More

Books

Baxter, Nicola. *Hot or Not?* Chicago: Childrens Press, 1996.

Fowler, Allan. *Hot and Cold*. Chicago: Childrens Press, 1994.

Ramsay, Helena. *Hot and Cold*. Illustrated by Andrew Farmer and Peter Bull. New York: Children's Press, 1998.

Web Sites

Brain Pop
www.brainpop.com/science/seeall.weml (click on "heat" or "temperature")

National Geographic
www.nationalgeographic.com/world/amfacts/why.html

Index

GR: I
Word Count: 256

From Alison Auch

Reading and writing are my favorite
things to do. When I'm not reading
or writing, I like to hike in the
mountains or play with my five cats!

24